HUMBLING THYSELF

Brenda B. Matthews

Bea-Mor Publishing

Copyright © 2002 Brenda B. Matthews

Revised 2020

ISBN-10 - 0989136833
ISBN-13 - 9780989136839

All Rights Reserved. No part of this book may be copied in any form to include electronically without the written permission of the author.

E-mail – brendabmatthews@att.net

All scriptures are taken from the King James Version of the Bible.

Editors:
Minister Josephine Johnson
Regina Ware
Lady Denise Battle

Printed in the United States of America

DEDICATION

I dedicate this book to all who have a desire to walk or to continuously walk in the spirit of humility. Many believe they are humble; many think they are humble, and many say they are. The truth is; it is what others believe, think, and say about you; not what you believe, think, or say.

PREFACE

If my people, which are called by my name, shall humble themselves, and pray, and seek my face, and turn from their wicked ways; then will I hear from heaven, and will forgive their sin, and will heal their land, 2 Chronicles 7:14

HUMILITY

Humility is one of the most needed spirits we "all" should possess.

Some will learn in-depth what humility is while others will have a broader understanding of the importance of humility.

WHAT IS HUMILITY?

Humility is the state of being lowly, modest, and lacking the spirit of haughtiness (pride).

Humility means that your heart, mind, and behavior are subject to God always. When Satan places a thought in your mind, your heart receives it, if you are caught off guard, but your spirit quickly intercedes and controls your behavior.

Example: During a business meeting, two ladies disagree. Though the disagreement was rectified, one lady is given a directive a week later by Satan to confront the lady in the presence of others. This was a perfect opportunity to belittle the other lady, which would make her stand tall in power and authority. As she formed her words to speak, she was given a greater directive by the Lord, through her spirit, to humble herself by not addressing the issue, but greeted her with kindness.

He who is humble, believes that in the eyes of God, he is an important individual, but in the eyes of himself, he is nothing. Not that his self-esteem is low, but his esteem for God is higher than the esteem he has for himself. Also, in the eyes of others, a humble man is the greatest, but in the eyes of himself, he is nothing.

A humble man has more compassion for others and their needs than for himself and his needs.

A humble man's prayer is directed in the intercessory arena more so than personal petition or requisition prayers. In essence, he prays for others and their needs before praying for himself and his needs.

A humble man speaks with his heart prior to speaking with his mouth. While conversing with this man of humility, the peace of God is immediately detected in his life and the listeners' mind is serene and pacified in a manner that constitutes no description.

A humble man places others before himself always. Others are more relevant to him than he is to himself. Example: A humble man will enter a building last, holding the door for everyone. A humble man will take the end of the line allowing all others to go ahead. A humble man will make sure everyone eats first. If there is not enough for him, he will eat something else later.

A humble man will seek and find positivity in the most negative scenario.

A humble man's quiet spirit is often taken for granted or mistaken for weakness. His words are few, but rich, tasteful, and satisfying.

The spirit of humility is often preached and taught by many; however, few learn it.

THE IMPORTANCE OF HUMILITY

Humility is the "only" way we can be used by God. When we say unto the Lord in prayer, "Use me as Your instrument or use me as Your tool," we need to know what that statement entails. When we speak these precious words, we are saying, "Lord, in whatever way You need me to help, no matter the time of day, no matter the weather, no matter what I think or believe, no matter the distance, no matter the need, no matter the individual or circumstance, I am available unto You." This is one who possesses the spirit of humility.

When we say unto the Lord in prayer, "Use me as Your instrument or use me as Your tool," but in our mind and heart we are saying, "As long as it is not early in the morning or late at night; as long as the weather is fair; as long as it is logical to me; as long as it is not too far; as long as it is in route to where I am going; as long as I am truly needed; as long as I like the person; and as long as the circumstance is not too overbearing for me, we are not fully available to God. Our prayer can be unto the Lord to use us as His instrument, but add, "Lord, I do want You to know that I have restrictions." Is this your behavior? Is this your prayer?

HOW TO POSSESS HUMILITY

In prayer, ask God to reveal to you your spirit.

Ask God to highlight instances when the spirit of humility transpired in your life and in the life of others.

Ask God to show you incidences where the spirit of humility was not presented in your life or in the life of others.

Ask God to overshadow you with the spirit of humility when you are engaged in conversations.

Ask God to manufacture or create situations for you so you can recognize the spirit of humility in individuals versus haughtiness. Ask Him to make it known to you that He created the circumstance so you could observe the matter and know that the spirit of humility was displayed.

Ask God to humble you because it is understood that we cannot be used in pride.

Also, during intercessory prayer, ask God to humble others.

Remember, Jesus operated in the spirit of humility always, study His miracles. Jesus did not have to use the little boy's fish and bread to feed the multitude. He was showing us that He could take a little and make a lot if our trust is in Him. Jesus had the ability to show off His power by issuing each person a full course meal with dessert, at the same time. He had the ability and the power to "pour" the meal down from Heaven as it was with manna.

If we are to be imitators of Jesus Christ, we must walk in His likeness. Ask God in prayer to lead and guide you in His pathway.

Each morning, say to the Lord, "Direct my speech, direct my

thoughts, direct my heart, and direct my walk in the spirit of humility today."

HOW TO MAINTAIN HUMILITY

SUBMIT – GIVE YOUR ALL TO JESUS – In everything we do, we must put our heart into it, Colossians 3. Since our strength comes from the Lord, we must show our appreciation by giving Him our best on our jobs, in our homes, with our marriage, time, money, witnessing, singing, preaching, teaching, studying, praying, consecration, meditation, conversation, and faithfulness.

TRUST JESUS WITH ALL THINGS – When your job, your marriage, your vehicle, your finances, your credit, your home, or your best friend fail, Jesus is nearby. No matter how dark your cloud is, Jesus will always and will be light. Jesus cannot be hidden in darkness, Psalms 139:11, 12. He is the creator of great lights. He made the sun to rule by day. He made the moon and stars to rule by night, Psalms 136:8, 9. It is He who light our candles and enlighten our darkness, Psalm 18:28. Jesus is the oil in our lamp. Whatever is praised more than Jesus is "your trust" and fault will be found in it; it will not be everlasting. Whatever is praised more than the Lord, will be removed from you, somehow. Our God is a jealous God, For thou shalt worship no other god: for the LORD, whose name *is* Jealous, *is* a jealous God, Exodus 34:14 and Deuteronomy 6:14-16. Do you spend more time washing your car or washing your heart? Do you spend more time talking to friends or talking to the Lord? Do you spend more time looking in the mirror at your outer beauty or your inner beauty? Do you spend more time planning to reach the corporate ladder or the spiritual ladder? There is no fault in Jesus, trust Him. He will be your strongest hold, your anchor, your guide, and He is Everlasting.

BELIEVE THE WORDS OF JESUS – Every word of God is pure, Proverbs 30:5. If Jesus says it, it must be believed. If we do not believe, we have no faith. If we have no faith, it is impossible to please Him, Hebrews 11:6.

ABIDE BY THE WORDS OF JESUS – Just to hear God's word or to be aware of God's word means little unless His word is abiding in us. When His word is abiding in us, we are able to ask the Lord whatever we choose and it shall be done unto us, John 15:7. When we preach, teach, witness, rear children, oversee a business, or pastor a church, prayer will get us through.

SPEAK THE WORDS OF JESUS – The word of God is quick and powerful, and sharper than any two-edged sword, Hebrews 4:12. Therefore, when we speak, sing, or pray, spirits are uplifted, yokes are broken, shackles are loosened, souls are saved, and more.

LIVE IN HOLINESS – Live according to the will, the ways, and the word of God.

The will of God – Speaking, moving, and doing what God says, when He says it, learning later what His reason or purpose was.

The ways of God – Replicating God (possessing all of God's attributes, but in a smaller denomination); duplicating God (looking exactly like God), and imitating God (looking and acting like God).

The word of God – Following God's commandments, statutes, and laws written in the Bible.

David asked, "Lord, who shall abide in thy tabernacle? Who shall dwell in thy holy hill?" David wanted to know who was going to Heaven. The Lord answered him in Psalms 15:1-5.

He that walketh uprightly; he does not sin purposely or knowingly. If he does, it is immediately acknowledged, then he repents. His desire is to walk with the Lord, pleasing Him daily.

He that worketh righteousness; all of his works are done in the pureness of heart continuously.

He that speaketh the truth in his heart; One can speak or preach the truth and not believe what is spoken. He who speaketh the truth in his heart is one who believes the truth first, then speaks it, continuously.

He that backbiteth not with his tongue; One who will not degrade others with his mouth.

He that doeth no evil to his neighbor.

He that does not taketh up a reproach against his neighbor; One who will not listen to others slander or gossip about his neighbor.

In whose eyes a vile person is contemned; One who views sin as sin, dirt as dirt, and a lie as a lie.

He honoureth them that fear the Lord; One who honors all men who serve God. He respects men because they are the sons of God. He admires men whose mind and spirit are anchored to the Lord. He knows that this man can reach Heaven in prayer and will intercede in prayer for him.

He sweareth to his own hurt and changeth not; One who keeps his promises; he keeps his word; he will hurt himself just to make his promise good and he will not change his mind. If he has to reschedule due to an unexpected circumstance, he will communicate with the party.

He that putteth not out his money to usury; One will not indulge in getting rich illegally. He will not invest his money in lotteries, casinos, animal races, or any unclean trading. He will not set up shops, legally draining the pockets of others, becoming rich later. He labors legally, earnestly, and honestly for his income and pays 10 percent of his earnings to God's house.

He that does not taketh up reward against the innocent; One who

will not overcharge struggling, innocent customers of merchandise in
neighborhood stores. He will not take advantage of songwriters, authors, and script writer's rights by offering deals on a contract, only to put the writers in debt.

Meditate on these verses and add them to your list of things to do to live in holiness!

ABSTAIN FROM FOOD AND PLEASURES FOR JESUS – When we give up something for God, He will give up something for us. To sacrifice food for one day for God is greater than sacrificing four years of college for ourselves. To hear one word from God is more worthy than hearing four years of words from college professors.

LOVE JESUS WHOLE-HEARTEDLY- When Jesus is loved from our heart, he hears our cry, He delivers us out of trouble, and He bestows blessings upon us. He opens doors for us that men try to close, and He grants us favor. He is our Divine Protector, Divine Sustainer, and Divine Shield.

SEEK THE FACE Of JESUS DAILY- My voice shalt thou hear in the morning, O Lord; in the morning will I direct my prayer unto thee, and will look up, Psalm 5:3. It is imperative that we retire for the evening with God on our mind and awaken with praises, speaking to and hearing from Him again.

SING TO AND FOR JESUS - We sometimes sing to our new born babies, our beautiful plants, and our significant other. Then we must remember to sing to Jesus; He delights in our praises; He loves to hear us sing to Him. When we are alone, that is when we are to speak to ourselves in psalms and hymns and spiritual songs, singing and making melody in our heart to the Lord, Ephesians 5:19. This is the time to be in the "spotlight" or on "Broadway", when we are alone! When singing, we are to sing "for" Jesus. Souls are saved, souls are delivered, shackles are loosened, yokes are broken, hearts are mended, and more when we sing "for" Jesus and "not for" ourselves.

PRAY FOR A CLOSER RELATIONSHIP WITH JESUS - Trials and Tribulations are the results of asking for a closer relationship with Jesus. During our storms, when anchored to Jesus, we are to praise, worship, fast, pray, consecrate, and meditate; this is called "Doing God's Will". Jesus will step into our troubles to comfort, direct, and mold us. We will trust Him more, depend on Him, and learn more about Him, this is called "Closeness".

STUDY THE BIBLE- Bible study differs from the study of books. When we study books, our aim is to remember what we have heard, read, or saw. Studying the bible is the meditation of scriptures read; in-depth thinking of scriptures heard; thinking of how the scriptures read or heard applies to our lives now and how we will apply them to our lives in the future. Study is the work of the mind; meditation is the work of the heart. During meditation (quiet time), we are resting scriptures upon our heart and within our heart. These rested or stored scriptures will automatically come to our mind when needed and will always be remembered. The mind cannot store as much information as the heart, it will begin a deletion process. The heart is ever ready to receive more, never stating," I have enough". Studying without meditation enables us to remember long enough to take "a" test. Studying with meditation enables us to remember long enough "through" tests. (Read page 95 for meditation suggestions)

PONDER SCRIPTURES IN YOUR HEART - When we meditate on scriptures, we are pondering scriptures in our heart. Pondered scriptures are relevant when witnessing, comforting others, and encouraging ourselves. It also helps us in our praying.

PRAY THE SCRIPTURES - When praying the scriptures, our prayers are fervent (real) and effectual (powerful). Praying the scriptures causes the walls of the sanctuary to shake and dead spirits to awaken.

SHARE THE BIBLE - Whenever given the opportunity, tell someone of the good news of the great gospel of Jesus Christ, His death, burial, and resurrection. Some may be familiar with Jesus' miracles; some may have heard about His power, but if you know Him, it is necessary to publish it with a loud voice.

PRAISE AND WORSHIP JESUS - Oh how Jesus is delighted when we praise Him; He loves to hear us discussing Him; He loves when we exalt Him, lifting Him up, and His name; He loves it when we place Him before all people and all things.

Praise is expressing heartily "in words or songs" or both a high opinion of Jesus Christ. Praise is speaking well of Jesus Christ by telling Him what He is to us and what He has done for us. Also, praise is an "act" of expressing that Jesus Christ is "good" with a dance, a shout, uplifted arms, clapping of the hands, lying prostrate, tears, moaning and groaning, speaking in other tongues, laughter, jumping, running and more.

We can all praise God with our lips; we can sound like we are praising God; we can look like we are praising God, and we can act like we are praising God; however, when we speak from our heart, Jesus is in the midst of our praise.

When praising God with our lips, (Example) Lord, You are so worthy, You are honorable, You are excellent, You have protected me, You have saved me, You have forgiven me, You have blessed me, etc. Believing in your heart the words of praise spoken by you, you begin to feel the Lord's presence; the doors of worship are opened.

Praise opens the door to Worship.

Worship is expressing who Jesus Christ is to us; it is personal adoration of Jesus Christ. (Example) Jesus is my peace of mind, my lifter up, my healer, my provider, my refuge, my light, my strength, etc.

When you feel the presence of God, you are in the state of worship. As you begin worshipping Jesus, you will feel His power all over you, that power is the "anointing". When you feel the anointing, anything you say will be of God because it is God working through you (you are under God's power). You will have "Holy" boldness (having the ability to speak to anyone, anywhere, anytime about Jesus); laying your hands on souls causing minds and hearts to change; causing the blind to see; the deaf to hear; the lame to walk. When the anointing comes into the place, it comes to do a work that man cannot do with his hands; the anointing comes to do a work that only Jesus Himself can.

Worship is intimately praising God; no one can worship the Lord for you, but one can worship the Lord with you. Some are able to bypass praise and move directly into worship because of their relationship with the Lord. If this is not you, know that it can be you.

DO YOUR ALL FOR JESUS IN EVERYTHING And whatsoever ye do in word or deed, do all in the name of the Lord Jesus, giving thanks to God and the Father by Him, Colossians 3:17. And whatsoever ye do, do it heartily, as to the Lord, and not unto men, Colossians 3:23.

HOW TO KNOW YOU ARE HUMBLE

Stay in the will of God. When we walk uprightly, our thinking, living, speaking, preaching, and teaching will be in holiness. In holiness, we imitate Jesus Christ, and as imitators, we follow His pathway. We listen for His voice, we wait for His instructions, we act like Him, and because He knows that we adore Him so much that we impersonate His great gospel, he sheds His light, His word, and His power upon us and within us we can carry out His work for Him.

Others recognize the spirit of humility in you, not you. They will inform <u>you</u> of your spirit.

Knowing that you endeavor to walk like Jesus in your spirit and not just with lip service, it is known to you by God that you do not possess the spirit of haughtiness. On the other hand, a humble man will not profess to be humble because he is not aware of his humility.

A humble man discerns the spirit of haughtiness in himself and in others. When it is discerned, he prays immediately, asking the Lord to cast out the spirit.

A humble man will not be heard saying, "I know I am humble, everybody knows I am." I define this spirit as "Boastfully Humble". I pray this is not you.

THE SPIRIT OF HAUGHTINESS

Haughtiness is an unclean spirit that causes individuals to be full of pride, arrogant, and conceited, showing excessive self-esteem.

Of course, God wants us to be happy about our personal accomplishments, our children and their accomplishments, our goals we have met, our lifestyles, our possessions, etc. God wants us to remember Him in all that we do and in all that we have. He blesses us so we can be a blessing to others and testify of His goodness to win souls. When we receive from God, not giving Him thanks, praise, or credit, it bothers Him. It bothers me, so I know it bothers Him. When we take blessings from God and boast about them, making others feel less fortunate, it bothers God. When we receive blessings from God and think we are greater than others or greater than the Creator, it bothers Him.

Haughtiness is pride, the exact opposite of humility.

Possessing the spirit of haughtiness, we limit ourselves from the blessings of God and we limit God from using His gifts through us. We want to be readily available to the Lord, and we can only be available when we are walking in the spirit of humility.

In pride, we are not available unto the Lord, but we are available unto Satan. In pride, we think "we" are the important one. We are swift to speak and slow to hear which is contrary to the Bible. Jesus was "swift" to hear and "slow" to speak. We think "we" are just as great, if not greater than God. We think highly of our accomplishments and look down on all who has little or nothing.

Possessing this spirit, how can we grow spiritually? We cannot grow because we know everything, and no one can tell us anything; we have all the answers. We do not need help with anything, and if we did, we have too much pride to call for help.

If _you_ possess this spirit, put this book down right now and say to God, "Lord, Your word tells me to humble myself. I am asking You to humble me in the name of Jesus." Be sure to ask God to humble you before He decides to humble you. And whosoever shall exalt himself shall be abased (humbled): and he that shall humble himself shall be exalted, Matthew 23:12.

Walking with assurance, speaking with Holy boldness, or possessing high self-esteem differs drastically from possessing the spirit of haughtiness, though sometimes mistaken as haughtiness. The difference is God's light gives us assurance to know that we are sowing seeds of righteousness, allowing us to witness the fruit we bear. God's word gives us Holy boldness to work for Him, fearing Him and not man, enabling us to stand firmly on His promises, sharing with others His promises. God's presence gives us self-esteem to move and speak by His power, His might, and His timing.

HOW TO RECOGNIZE HUMILITY

View the thoughts and behavior of a haughty man versus the thoughts and behavior of a humble man. The haughty man and the humble man in this analogy are MINISTERS. Substitute MINISTER with the title you personally hold to see where you stand.

THE HAUGHTY MINISTER believes he can preach well.

THE HUMBLE MINISTER believes he is not the best preacher.

THE HAUGHTY MINISTER believes he is knowledgeable.

THE HUMBLE MINISTER believes he knows not enough.

THE HAUGHTY MINISTER believes he has studied the Bible enough.

THE HUMBLE MINISTER believes he needs more study time.

THE HAUGHTY MINISTER enjoys the attention from others as he speaks.

THE HUMBLE MINISTER wants to hide "self" so that he is not seen as he speaks and desire God's presence, so the listeners are touched.

THE HAUGHTY MINISTER loves crowds; the more people, the better. A crowd makes him feel like a king; he can really show off.

THE HUMBLE MINISTER believes that if two or three are gathered together, Jesus is in the midst.

THE HAUGHTY MINISTER works for rewards from people.

THE HUMBLE MINISTER works for God "only".

THE HAUGHTY MINISTER believes that if no one comes to the

altar to be saved, then so what. "Everyone else enjoyed me, stood up for me, applauded for me, shouted, and I received my honorarium, my offering." His aim is to please man as it looks as if he is pleasing God.

THE HUMBLE MINISTER believes that if one soul comes "not" to the altar to be saved, he consults God with a bleeding heart. He cannot rest and neither can he sleep that night. His aim is to win souls as he pleases God.

THE HAUGHTY MINISTER trusts in the riches that come from God.

THE HUMBLE MINISTER trusts in God and God's riches.

THE HAUGHTY MINISTER prays for more materials from God (home, vehicle, finances, jewelry, clothing, etc.).

THE HUMBLE MINISTER prays for more material from God (revelation, wisdom, knowledge, understanding, scriptures, sermons, clichés, stories, greater speaking techniques, books, mentors, fasting and praying regimens, etc.).

THE HAUGHTY MINISTER enters a church, automatically heading to the front row of the church or the pulpit.

THE HUMBLE MINISTER takes a seat in the back of the church until asked or escorted further.

THE HAUGHTY MINISTER puts down other minister's preaching style, preaching techniques, or presentation to build up himself.

THE HUMBLE MINISTER builds up other ministers by praying about their preaching style, preaching techniques, or presentations, which also builds up himself.

THE HAUGHTY MINISTER boasts of his power.

THE HUMBLE MINISTER cries unto the Lord for more of His power.

THE HAUGHTY MINISTER speaks of "ME, MY, and I" sharing with others about what he has, what he had, and what he is getting; where he was, where he is, and where he is going.

THE HUMBLE MINISTER "IF HE SPEAKS", he speaks of things God is doing, what God has done, and what God will do. He accepts no glory and neither does he take any glory. Glory belongs to God!

THE HAUGHTY MINISTER is asked a question, "Who wants to preach?" He answers, "I will!"

THE HUMBLE MINISTER is asked a question, "Who wants to preach?" He answers not a word.

THE HAUGHTY MINISTER tells all. He utters all his mind.

THE HUMBLE MINISTER is discreet. A fool utters all his mind, but a wise man keepeth it in till afterwards, Proverbs 29:11.

THE HAUGHTY MINISTER debates scriptures.

THE HUMBLE MINISTER discusses scriptures.

THE HAUGHTY MINISTER drags men in to hear him preach and to see him.

THE HUMBLE MINISTER draws men to the Lord.

THE HAUGHTY MINISTER looks to see what he has done in the services and during the services.

THE HUMBLE MINISTER looks to see what God has done in the services and during the services.

THE HAUGHTY MINISTER lifts up himself, exalting himself.

THE HUMBLE MINISTER lifts up God, exalting God.

THE HAUGHTY MINISTER imitates men.

THE HUMBLE MINISTER imitates God.

THE HAUGHTY MINISTER believes that in times of competition, he cannot be beat, and he will not be beat; he must win.

THE HUMBLE MINISTER believes that in times of competition, he will not enter the contest.

THE HAUGHTY MINISTER professes to be humble; believes he is humble; boasts of his humility to others, and no one ever tells him he is humble.

THE HUMBLE MINISTER knows not that he is humble but knows that he is not haughty. The thought of haughtiness disturbs his spirit. When haughtiness seems to be present, he asks God to cast it out instantaneously. Oh, others tell him he is humble, and his spirit is discussed amongst others.

THE HAUGHTY MINISTER handles criticism defensively. He defends himself quickly, puts folk in their rightful places regardless of the truth or untruth of the criticism.

THE HUMBLE MINISTER handles criticism defenselessly. If the criticism is true, he asks God for peace, direction, understanding, comfort, forgiveness, etc. If the criticism is untrue, he knows that his Christian walk is upright because Satan is causing disruption.

THE HAUGHTY MINISTER goes first.

THE HUMBLE MINISTER allows others to go first.

THE HAUGHTY MINISTER takes a stand quickly.

THE HUMBLE MINISTER takes a seat quickly.

THE HAUGHTY MINISTER gives up easily (throwing in the towel).

THE HUMBLE MINISTER gives it to God easily.

THE HAUGHTY MINISTER loves himself and God.

THE HUMBLE MINISTER loves God, then himself.

THE HAUGHTY MINISTER takes care of himself, then home.

THE HUMBLE MINISTER takes care of home, then himself.

THE HAUGHTY MINISTER looks over the problem by ignoring the problem or avoiding the problem.

THE HUMBLE MINISTER looks through the problem (meditating/waiting on a word from God). He looks past the problem (exercises faith). He looks into the problem (weighs out the pros and cons). He looks at the problem (faces the matter).

THE HAUGHTY MINISTER wants your life changed so he can be glorified.

THE HUMBLE MINISTER wants your life changed so God can be glorified.

THE HAUGHTY MINISTER takes charge.

THE HUMBLE MINISTER takes care.

THE HAUGHTY MINISTER's chest and head swells.

THE HUMBLE MINISTER heart swells.

THE HAUGHTY MINISTER sits high and looks low.

THE HUMBLE MINISTER sits low and looks high.

THE HAUGHTY MINISTER looks at God, for he knows that he and God are on the same level.

THE HUMBLE MINISTER looks up to God, for he knows he is beneath God.

THE HAUGHTY MINISTER serves as a great king.

THE HUMBLE MINISTER serves "the" Great King, Jesus.

THE HAUGHTY MINISTER is wise in his own eyesight, always boasting and bragging of his wisdom.

HUMBLING THYSELF

THE HUMBLE MINISTER knows not that he is wise; others tell him he is. Others always want to talk with him just to learn from him.

THE HAUGHTY MINISTER signifies when he prays.

<u>THE HUMBLE MINISTER edifies when he prays.</u>

THE HAUGHTY MINISTER thinks everyone wants to be like him. He thinks everyone is jealous of him, his accomplishments, and his possessions.

THE HUMBLE MINISTER knows "not" that others desire to be like him. He knows "not" that the light of Jesus Christ overshadows him as he touches many lives, and he dwells not on his accomplishments or possessions.

THE HAUGHTY MINISTER studies to shew himself that he can prove.

THE HUMBLE MINISTER studies to shew himself approved.

THE HAUGHTY MINISTER thinks, believes, and knows he is powerful.

THE HUMBLE MINISTER is powerful.

THE HAUGHTY MINISTER sings to win contests.

THE HUMBLE MINISTER sings to win souls.

THE HAUGHTY MINISTER prays intellectually to man, expecting praise for his great selection of words.

THE HUMBLE MINISTER prays sincerely to God, praising and expecting a great collection of blessings.

THE HAUGHTY MINISTER pretends to be Holy; he looks Holy; he sounds Holy, and he dresses Holy.

THE HUMBLE MINISTER is Holy.

THE HAUGHTY MINISTER sees with his eyes.

THE HUMBLE MINISTER sees with his heart.

THE HAUGHTY MINISTER takes.

THE HUMBLE MINISTER gives.

THE HAUGHTY MINISTER gives up.

THE HUMBLE MINISTER gives in.

THE HAUGHTY MINISTER cares not.

THE HUMBLE MINISTER cares for.

THE HAUGHTY MINISTER dictates.

THE HUMBLE MINISTER advises.

THE HAUGHTY MINISTER hears.

THE HUMBLE MINISTER listens.

THE HAUGHTY MINISTER preys on the weak.

THE HUMBLE MINISTER prays for the weak.

THE HAUGHTY MINISTER feels hurt.

THE HUMBLE MINISTER feels others hurt.

THE HAUGHTY MINISTER's words are hard as gold.

THE HUMBLE MINISTER's words are pure as gold.

THE HAUGHTY MINISTER's ways are hard as sugar cane.

THE HUMBLE MINISTER's ways are sweet as sugar cane.

THE HAUGHTY MINISTER's thoughts are pleasing to himself.

THE HUMBLE MINISTER's thoughts are pleasing to God.

THE HAUGHTY MINISTER follows his plan without hesitation.

THE HUMBLE MINISTER follow God's plan without hesitation.

THE HAUGHTY MINISTER is submissive to his authority.

THE HUMBLE MINISTER is submissive to authority.

THE HAUGHTY MINISTER compares himself to the lives of others.

THE HUMBLE MINISTER compares himself to the life of Jesus Christ.

My prayer is that you were touched by the layout above, Haughtiness versus Humility. I pray that your understanding of humility is clearer. Also, you should be able to better recognize the two spirits in yourself and within others.

A STORY OF PRIDE AND HUMILITY

One day a great ruler of old was resting in his home, flourishing in his palace. He had a dream that frightened him and the understanding of it was unclear. The thoughts and visions of the dream troubled him.

The ruler then called for the wise men to interpret the dream, but they were unable to. He then called on a Holy man to interpret the dream; a man who fasted and prayed; a man who consecrated himself; a man who was in constant meditation; a man who was faithful to God; and a man who was trusted by God.

God gave the Holy man the interpretation of the ruler's dream. The purpose of the dream was to inform the ruler that God "was" and "is" the supreme Ruler regardless to what man acquires, thinks, or feels. The ruler was prosperous and had power over men. God had to show him who was greater and who is the greatest. God wanted him to know that all power comes from Him (power of the people, power for the people, power upon the people, power in the people, power through the people, and power over the people) and that power comes "not" from man. He wanted the ruler to know that it is "He" who exalts men and "He" who bring men low. If we remember nothing else, God wants us to know that He is the King of His Kingdom and the King of our kingdom.

God not only showed the ruler His plan in the dream, He showed it to him by manifestation.

The Holy man shared the interpretation of the dream with the ruler. After 12 months, the ruler experienced the interpretation of the dream by manifestation.

The ruler must have forgotten about the dream he had a year prior. One day, he was walking in his palace, boasting of the greatness of his kingdom, built by the might of "his" power. As he was speaking, a voice from Heaven fell saying, "The kingdom is departed from thee, and they shall drive thee from men, and thy dwelling place shall be with the beasts of the field. They shall make thee to eat grass as oxen (cattle), and seven times (seven years) shall pass over thee until thou know that the Most High ruleth in the kingdom of men, and giveth it to whomsoever he will."

In the same hour, the manifestation transpired. The ruler was driven from men; he lost his throne. He was given the heart of a beast. He ate grass as oxen. His body was wet with the dew of Heaven. His hair grew like eagle's feathers, and his nails grew like bird's claws.

When the ruler realized who **was** and who **is** King, he lifted up his eyes unto Heaven; his understanding returned unto him. He blessed the Most High. He praised and honored Him that liveth forever, whose dominion is an everlasting dominion and His Kingdom is from generation to generation. He then knew that all the inhabitants (people) of the earth were reputed (considered) as nothing. It was then that he realized God does things according to His will in the army of Heaven and no one can stop Him or no one can say to Him, "What are you doing, God?"

At the same time the ruler's reason returned unto him, the glory of his kingdom, his honor and brightness was returned unto him. His counselors and lords sought unto him. He was established in his kingdom and excellent majesty was added unto him.

The ruler said that he will praise, extol, and honor the King of Heaven, all whose works are truth, His ways judgment, and those that walk in pride He is able to abase (bring low).

This is a true story in Daniel, Chapter IV. The ruler's name is king Nebuchadnezzar. The wise men were the astrologers, magicians, Chaldeans, and soothsayers. The dream interpreter was Daniel, whose name was Belteshazzar, and of course the supreme King is God.

Because the ruler had so many possessions and authority, operating in the spirit of haughtiness, he was not aware of his sins. He could not hear God and he did not have time to live for God.

Sometimes we get too busy to pray, too busy to praise, and too busy to serve God. God has a way of making us "make" and "take" time to pray, praise, and serve, such as it was with the king.

Remember that your kingdom is not higher than God's Kingdom. When you think it is, God can and God will deliver you from foolish thinking. <u>Your KINGDOM (**your ministry, your company, your investments, your savings, your title, your position, your name, your possessions, etc.**</u>) is not too high, whereas God cannot and will not tear it down.

It does not matter whom we are, what authority over people we have, what town we reside in, what our educational level is, what franchise we own, what we possess, or what our last name is, God is our Divine Ruler. He does the building up of kings and kingdoms and He tears them down too.

THE PROCESS OF BECOMING HUMBLE

Live in holiness – By believing God's word; studying God's word; pondering God's word in your heart, mind, and spirit; abiding by God's word, meditating on God's word, and spreading God's word.

Let your light shine – Let your light so shine before men, that they may see your good works, and glorify your Father which is in heaven, Matthew 5:16.

Look to God for all things – Consult God in all areas of your life. Seek help from God with your marriage, employment, thoughts, family, health, finances, disappointments, decisions, discouragement, and more.

Love God – Exalt Him at all times in spite of your difficulties. Remember that God is over our problems just as He is over the world. It must be believed and known that the higher we lift God, the lower our difficulty becomes.

Learn to bridle your tongue – Ask God to help you select the words to speak. All things are lawful for me, but all things are not expedient; all things are lawful for me, but all things edify not, 1 Corinthians 10:23.

Lean not unto thine own understanding – Trust God whole heartedly. Worry not about why you are troubled or why folk trouble you. Remember, you are Humbling Thyself!

List your priorities – God, others, and then self. Let nothing be done through strife or vainglory; but in lowliness of mind let each esteem other better than themselves. Look not every man on his own things, but every man also on the things of others, Philippians 2:3, 4.

Let others, who are full of wisdom, correct you and direct you when needed. Remember, those who love us and care about us are only protecting us from future failure and directing us in present problems. We cannot think we know it all, and we should not be angry with those who attempt to help us.

Lower yourselves when with others. Though you may have an impressive title, when with others, discuss matters irrelevant to the job, when away from the job. Always make people feel as if they can relate to you. Whatever title you hold, always make co-workers feel that you are nothing without God. Remember, if you come down low enough and stay down low enough, you will hear a word from Jesus.

Lavish over the power that is in Jesus' name. Lavish over His presence, His love, His promises, and His life always.

Lift your voice to speak beneath Jesus, not above Him. Speak, knowing that all of your direction, guidance, and help comes from the Lord; not self. Speak knowing that when we boast and brag about what we have, what we are getting, where we are going, where we have been, what we have done, what we are doing, etc., God hears us and He is in the process of snatching it back. God wants us to give Him honor for all that we have and all that we do. Speak knowing that God is the Most High and we are the most low; regardless to our backgrounds, education, honors, titles, experiences, finances, where we reside, or the make and model of our cars. When we exalt ourselves, great strength is required. When we do this, we do not have as much strength to come down. Since God's strength is great, He will handle it for us, He will bring us down; He will humble us with no problem. God is no respecter of persons. If we walk in the spirit of humility, we will automatically speak beneath Jesus (in humility). We cannot speak to people as if we are greater than them or as if they are beneath us. The message that we are trying to convey to them will not be received. We have to assure our listeners that we are all riding on the same boat (share testimonies), singing the same song (share struggles or issues you are faced with at home). This way, their mind is open to receive the Word from us. We are as a blade of grass and a withered flower. The voice said, Cry. And he said, What shall I cry? All flesh is grass, and all the goodliness thereof is as the flower of the field. The grass withereth, the flower fadeth: because the spirit of the Lord bloweth upon it: surely the people is grass. The grass withereth, the flower fadeth: but the word of our God shall stand for ever, Isaiah 40:6-8. We too, are as filthy rags. But we are all as an unclean thing, and all our righteousnesses are as filthy rags; and we all do fade as a leaf; and our iniquities, like the wind, have taken us away, Isaiah 64:6. We are not to present ourselves as greater than or more important than others as we speak for the Lord. Listeners should know that we speak beneath Jesus; not above Him.

Lay prostrate before God in prayer and in any prayer position you desire. Remember, there is power in prayer.

In prayer, always ask God to clothe you in humility or to keep you clothed in humility. When we possess the spirit of humility, we can be used mightily by God. Humility is the only way we can be used by God.

It is not easy 'Humbling Thyself' and it is not easy becoming humble. The attributes required in becoming humble are "pain" and "suffering." These attributes not only humble us, but they help us maintain the spirit of humility; they strengthen us. We then become anointed because our dependence is solely upon Jesus. We await direction and correction from Him. So, when we speak, it will be Jesus speaking through us. When we move, it will be Jesus moving through us. When we write, it will be Jesus writing through us. He will get the credit; he will get the glory.

Pain and suffering or trials and tribulations, we all must endure according to the Holy Bible. Yea and all that will live godly in

Christ Jesus shall suffer persecution, 2 Timothy 3:12.

Jesus suffered and died for our sins. He died with our sins upon Him. Therefore, we no longer have to live in sin, but we can die to sin and live in holiness. Jesus lived to die to rise again. When He arose, He had all power in His hands. As imitators of Jesus, we live for Him, suffering, trusting, and with power, then we die in Him, and rise again with Him.

In our suffering, we must be anchored to Jesus Christ, our solid Rock, to possess peace, strength, and His power. The power of Jesus is the anointing. Do not be quick to ask God to deliver you from or out of your troubles. Invite Him into comfort and direct you. When we desire the easy way out (immediate deliverance), we sometimes miss the lesson that God wants us to learn.

A learned lesson and great pain, with many tears, prayers, and patience is great gain!

MEDITATION

Meditation - Contemplating in quietness; taking the word of God you have just read or the scriptures just memorized, applying them to your personal life to enhance your spiritual life in seclusion, while waiting to hear the voice of God. Remember, when we are praying all of the time, talking to God, we must find quiet time to hear from God. This is done during meditation time. Not saying that this is the only time God speaks to us, but meditation time allows us to set aside all other things just for God to speak to us. Meditation time is a blessing for both you and God. It is a blessing for you because you will hear directly from our Savior. It is a blessing for God because you, His child, made preparation, a sacrifice, just for Him to speak to you. There is nothing more special than a father and child spending time together!

Meditation can and will take place while driving alone in our vehicles, while in the restroom, while walking; while working; anywhere in quietness.

Stand in awe, and sin not: commune with your own heart upon your bed, and be still. Selah, Psalm 4:4. Suggestion: During meditation time, listen to the flowing of water. If you have a portable water fountain, allow the water to flow as you are still. If you do not have one, allow your kitchen faucet to run as you meditate. Turn the restroom faucets on as soon as you enter, keeping them on the entire duration of your stay.

WHY?

BECAUSE YOU WILL HEAR THE VOICE OF THE LORD!

The voice of the Lord is upon the waters; the God of glory thundereth: the LORD is upon many waters, Psalm 29:3.

When we pray, we are doing the speaking: but when we meditate, God does the speaking and His voice will be heard upon the waters! If we are doing all of the speaking (praying), all of the time, when will we listen, how can we hear God, and when will we hear Him?

As in ordinary conversations, one speaks as the other listens; so it is with God. We both cannot speak at the same time. When we pray, we must make time to meditate.

After prayer, make time to hear from God. Just as we want to hear from God, He wants to speak to us. We sometimes do all of the talking, wondering why God has not answered our prayers. He tries to answer us, but as soon as He opens His mouth, we cut Him off to answer the phone, handle chores, deal with the kids, run an errand, and so on. We then pray again, cut God off again, and pray again. We think we are exercising faith as we are waiting, but our answer is at hand or was at hand; our ears were not.

Practice listening to the voice of the Lord; it is powerful! The more time spent listening for His voice, the more you will hear His voice. The more you hear His voice, the greater desire you will have to hear it and the more time you will allot to hear it.

When speaking in tongues, you are praying in the Spirit, speaking mysteries to God, For he that speaketh in an unknown tongue speaketh not unto men, but unto God: for no man understandeth him; howbeit in the spirit he speaketh mysteries, 1 Corinthians 14:2. Then ask the Lord for interpretation of the tongues spoken, 1 Corinthians 14:13.

WHO IS NAVIGATING YOU?

If we were in the market to purchase a navigation system and Google it, the results would be many. Whichever one we select, regardless to the features, brand or cost, expect malfunctions at some point. Some navigation systems will direct us to dead end streets and road construction, providing no detour info. Some will not warn us of accidents ahead, traffic, nor inclement weather.

New systems include an owner's manual which outlines directions, capabilities, warnings, and warranties. The underlined meaning of warranty is, do not trust the device, trust us to repair or replace the device; that is anticipated damage.

If you need to reach your destination, navigating through traffic, bad weather, dead end streets and construction detours in peace and on time, I recommend the ultimate navigation system, Jesus. He will guide you and never leave you unless you want to be left. He will guide you and keep you if you want to be kept. He will guide your mind, so your thoughts are established by Him. He will guide your eyes so you will see in the spirit. He will guide your tongue so you can call upon Him in times of trouble. He will guide your hands so you will sow your way out of financial ditches, and He will guide you to lay them upon the sick for recovery. He will guide your lips so you will speak His Word boldly. He will strengthen your legs so when He guides your feet, you can run through troops of trouble and leap over walls of tribulation as deer. The Lord maketh our feet as hinds' feet and sets us up in our **high places**, Psalm 18:33.

As we follow this system, nothing will be able to block us or stop us. Jesus will guide us through the fire, and we shall not burn. As a matter of fact, He will step in the fire with us as He did the Hebrew boys. He will guide us in the flood, and we will not be overtaken. **High places** mean protection from trouble and protection in trouble. Protection from trouble is when the Lord guides us above our dilemmas as the eagle that soars swiftly over storms. Because we are looking unto the hills from whence cometh our help, trusting Him, the Lord will spread His pavilion over us. He sets us **up upon** a rock, lifting us above our enemies. Setting us **up upon** a rock differs from setting us **upon** a rock. When we are set **upon** a rock, we are not easily seen by the enemy because we are on their level, but when we are set **up upon** a rock, we are seen by the enemy, not in pride, but with boldness. This allows the enemy's fiery darts to hit us and the rock we are set **up upon** is Jesus, Psalm 27. When the Lord sets us **up upon** a rock, we are sitting pretty high. Therefore, we are not afraid, Jesus is our salvation rock; He is our strength. This means we cannot fall; we shall stand and not be moved. We are standing on the promises of the Lord firmly. The protection in trouble is the Lord guiding us, pivoting our feet as deer through persecution in peace that surpasses understanding. No one will understand how we smile in our darkest hour and how we laugh when trouble is coming like a whirlwind. We should be able to say, "Jesus is the light and because He resides in me along with His Word, I am guided by Him. He is my navigator." The Word is a lamp unto our feet and a light unto our path, Psalm 119:105.

Choose Jesus as your navigation system. He has the best features; He is affordable; He has guarantees, not warranties; He is Everlasting; He will never go out of style; He has a brand name that shall be known by all. Guess what else? You can Google Jesus, but you cannot purchase Him. If your manual is not the Bible and you are not guided by the Word, then who is navigating you?

Allowing Jesus to navigate us; not we ourselves is humility. When we act as our own navigation system, we are operating in the spirit of pride.

CONCLUSION

If you were not enlightened while reading my book thus far, trust my final statement:

Satan will only attack areas in your life that will affect your spirit. Anything affecting your spiritual growth; affecting your prayer; affecting your marriage; affecting your home; affecting your emotions; affecting your finances; affecting your Bible study; and meditation time with God is a visit from the enemy (Satan). Remember, the visit from the enemy is just a test:

To see if you are going to operate in the spirit of humility or if you are going to operate in the spirit of haughtiness.

To make you **humble** or **haughty.**

A humble man has no time to wonder if he is humble or not. His endeavor is to keep God before him, above him, and over his life, his spirituality, his decisions, his home, his family, his finances, his job, his company, his marriages, etc. A man of humility is consistently humbling himself before God, but to say he is humble, he will never utter.

When God is given all of the honor, all of the glory, and all of the credit for all that you do, for all that you have done, for all that you say, for all that you have said, for all that you have, and for all that you have had, this places you in the state of **"HUMBLING THYSELF."**

One Point to Remember: If you ever believe that you have finally reached the goal of becoming humble, it is prayer time for you. Though others may tell you that you are humble, praise, honor, and glory go to God. Your response should be "Thank you for sharing that with me," and then thank God. When we see the face of

Jesus Christ in Heaven, even then, we will not be in a position to say, "I am humble". We will be able to say, "I was a humble person on Earth". Whatever desires you have, goals set, titles you hold, possessions acquired, or knowledge you have gained, know that you must always be in the state of **HUMBLING THYSELF!**

EXALT GOD

Thine, O Lord is the greatness, and the power, and the glory, and the victory, and the majesty: for all that is in the heaven and in the earth is thine; thine is the kingdom, O Lord, and thou art exalted as head above all, I Chronicles 29:11.

GOD WILL EXALT YOU

And all the trees of the field shall know that I the Lord have brought down the high tree, have exalted the low tree, have dried up the green tree, and have made the dry tree to flourish: I the Lord have spoken and have done it.

SCRIPTURAL REFERENCES (HUMILITY)

He hath shewed thee, O man, what is good; and what doth the LORD require of thee, but to do justly, and to love mercy, and to walk humbly with thy God? Micah 6:8.

And whosoeuer shall exalt himself, shall be abased: and he that shall humble himself, shall be exalted, Matthew 23:12.

Humble yourselves in the sight of the Lord, and he shall lift you up, James 4:10.

Likewise, ye younger, submit yourselves unto the elder. Yea, all of you be subject one to another, and be clothed with humility: for God resisteth the proud, and giveth grace to the humble, 1 Peter 5:5.

Humble yourselves therefore under the mighty hand of God, that he may exalt you in due time, 1 Peter 5:6.

Before destruction the heart of man is haughty, and before honour is humility, Proverbs 18:12.

A man's pride shall bring him low: but honour shall uphold the humble in spirit, Proverbs 29:23.

For thus saith the high and lofty One that inhabiteth eternity, whose name is Holy; I dwell in the high and holy place, with him also that is of a contrite and humble spirit, to revive the spirit of the humble, and to revive the heart of the contrite ones, Isaiah 57:15.

SCRIPTURAL REFERENCES (HAUGHTINESS)

The lofty looks of man shall be humbled, and the haughtiness of men shall be bowed down, and the Lord alone shall be exalted in that day, Isaiah 2:11.

Behold, the Lord, the Lord of hosts, shall lop the bough with terror: and the high ones of stature shall be hewn down, and the haughty shall be humbled, Isaiah 10:33.

And I will punish the world for their evil, and the wicked for their iniquity; and I will cause the arrogancy of the proud to cease, and will lay low the haughtiness of the terrible, Isaiah 13:11.

The earth mourneth and fadeth away, the world languisheth and fadeth away, the haughty people of the earth do languish, Isaiah 24:4.

Pride goeth before destruction, and an haughty spirit before a fall, Proverbs 16:18.

And they were haughty, and committed abomination before me: therefore, I took them away as I saw good, Ezekiel 16:50.

The wicked, through the pride of his countenance, will not seek after God: God is not in all his thoughts, Psalm 10:4.

In that day shalt thou not be ashamed for all thy doings, wherein thou hast transgressed against me: for then I will take away out of the midst of thee them that rejoice in thy pride, and thou shalt no more be haughty because of my holy mountain, Zephaniah 3:11.